THE CONCERTO

1800–1900

A Norton Music Anthology

Also by Paul Henry Lang

THE CONCERTO

1800-1900

A Norton Music Anthology

EDITED BY

PAUL HENRY LANG

W · W · NORTON & COMPANY · INC ·
New York

PRINTED IN THE UNITED STATES OF AMERICA

1 2 3 4 5 6 7 8 9 0

Contents

Preface

The Concerto in the Nineteenth Century

Next to opera, the concerto was the most original and significant contribution of the Italian Baroque to musical history. It soon spread, under Italian auspices, to Germany, France, and England, and by the end of the eighteenth century these four countries were producing a staggering number of concertos [1] of all descriptions, with solo instruments ranging from piccolo to double bass. A forthcoming companion anthology will be devoted to this rich and rewarding species of music, which counts among its leading masters Albinoni, Corelli, Vivaldi, Geminiani, Tartini, Bach and his sons, Handel, Mozart, Haydn, Boccherini, and a host of others.

As the Baroque concerto was constituted, the principal movement usually had four tuttis interspersed with solos, though this ratio was sometimes varied. This is called a ritornel concerto, the recurring tuttis or ritornels being not unlike the theme in a rondo. The alternation of solo and tutti was the essential feature of the concerto, and the great composers could sharpen the contrast and "competition" so that every return of the tutti seemed irresistible and inevitable. Solo and tutti had their own thematic material, enhancing the competitive, "concertante" or "concertizing" spirit and tone created by the discrepancy in the numbers of players and the contrasting dynamics. Near the middle of the eighteenth century, the concerto gradually turns its back on the robust Baroque forms and sounds, on the vigorous rhythms and syncopations; shortly after the middle of the century, the new sonata *idea* (which we somewhat restrictively call sonata *form*) began to invade all genres of music, and therewith the concerto. The sonata-symphony was based on the principle

[1] The Italian term *concerto* was borrowed by the English language early in the eighteenth century, and our present-day practice of using the Italian plural *concerti* within an English context is a bit affected. A glance at the title pages of early eighteenth-century publications in London will show that "concertos" was the accepted usage more than two hundred years ago. It is of course quite correct to use the Italian plural in *concerti grossi*, though the English in Handel's time preferred the English equivalent, "grand concertos." Similarly, "concerted" and "concertante" are fully acclimatized terms.

of tonal and thematic dualism; it too was a confrontation—and a highly dramatic one—between two antithetical tonalities, the opposition reinforced by equally antithetical themes, which entered into conflict that in the end had to be resolved in favor of the principal key. How could the two, concerto and symphony, be reconciled? The problem, as always, was to effect a judicious agreement between idiom, medium, and form—except that in the concerto the idiom itself was two-dimensional, technical virtuosity claiming an unusually large share in the musical convolutions. To combine real "concertizing" with bona fide symphonic construction was an aim and ideal that few have attained on a high artistic plane. The concertante elements evolved quite naturally in the ritornel concerto of the Baroque, but now the same competitive spirit had to be maintained within a different framework—a framework, as we have just said, in itself based on competition of a quite different sort.

Clearly, a compromise had to be made, for sonata construction did not permit the stereotyped solo-tutti alternation of the ritornel concerto; the solo part had to be coordinated with the orchestra in the joint symphonic elaboration of the thematic material. Nevertheless, the first composers of the concerto-symphony tried to retain the solo-tutti competition —which, not illogically, they considered the very raison d'être of the concerto—and hit upon the idea of giving each component a more or less full sonata exposition. This clashed, however, with logic and continuity, and with the modulatory scheme of the sonata structure. The compromise has been called by historians a "double exposition," though it is more nearly an "interrupted" or "divided" one. The first tutti was indeed an exposition, but it ended, contrary to the requirements of the sonata scheme, on the tonic, so that the solo could enter and it too could present the material, appropriately embellished with virtuoso appurtenances. Only after both partners had their say was the mandatory dominant (or relative major) key reached with a positive ending. This caused difficulties in the recapitulation, where everything must be reconciled with the tonic, of which already too much was present in the exposition. Only in the development section could the composer freely blend solo and tutti and remain faithful to both the concerto and the symphony. The question of how to make this double or divided exposition and its proper reprise logically feasible haunted every composer up to and including Brahms, and it is the eternal glory of Beethoven, Mendelssohn, Schumann, and Brahms that each in his own way found solutions which, though still carrying the marks of a compromise, resulted in great masterpieces. Only that wondrous genius, Mozart, was not troubled by the dilemma, for his Apollonian nature never had to wrestle with matter.

He accepted everything as he found it and then by some inexplicable alchemy made it his own; every problem was solved before it could be posed.

As the nineteenth century opened, public musical life was growing by leaps and bounds. Until this time, in most instances, the composer was his own performer; but now, with the establishment of organized concerts, the traveling virtuoso began his spectacular rise. The public wanted a display of virtuosity and the composers tried to satisfy this demand. The modern hammer piano, with its vastly improved sonorities and extended keyboard, now became powerful enough to stand up to the orchestra; the contrast became sharper because the piano's characteristic tone does not readily merge with that of the orchestra. A new style and technique of writing was required, and now the piano "specialist" appears, who like the earlier Italian and French violin composers wrote exclusively or mainly for one instrument. This tendency was to reach its culmination in Chopin and Liszt, surrounded by innumerable other pianist-composers. The violin, unless its part is carefully kept in the foreground and composed in the expansive concertante manner, will merge with the violins of the orchestra, while on the other hand, in slow movements, or when climbing far above the range of the accompanying instruments, its warm and soaring tone makes it an ideal vehicle for the concerto. Given this difference between the two instruments, we must deal separately with the two main types of the solo concerto.

❊ ❊ ❊

The eighteenth-century heritage was not well absorbed by the rising Romantic school. One of Mozart's original ways of dealing with the solo-tutti relationship within a symphonic ground plan while yet retaining the concerto character was to give the solo instrument rich figurations and passage work while the orchestra continues with the thematic-symphonic elaboration. Beethoven followed in Mozart's footsteps, and so did Johann Nepomuk Hummel (1778–1837), his great contemporary rival, an able composer even if manifestly not in Beethoven's class. Hummel's craftsmanship was of the finest, and his brilliant pianistic technique, both in writing and in playing, earned him the acclaim of all Europe. Yet in his otherwise attractive and still viable compositions we can already see what will later happen to the concerto in the hands of all but a few: the virtuoso finery gains the upper hand at the expense of compositional unity. Most composers become so enamored of the new Romantic piano tone that all their attention is riveted on the searching out of its possibilities. The passage work is now bedecked with runs in octaves or parallel thirds and sixths, there are sweeping runs encompassing the entire range of the keyboard, the piano opposes ringing chords to the full orchestra, and all kinds of novel effects are created by the equally novel pedal technique. The solo part is virtually independent of the thematic material, and not infrequently even of the formal concept of the work. Composers tried to grapple with the difficult problems of the concerto, but either they could not free themselves from the sonata-like construction, usually getting mired in conventional patterns, or, if they did escape, they lost cohesion. It is the more admirable that Mendelssohn and Brahms, staying altogether within the Classical, Beethovenian scheme, were able to create enduring and very personal concertos. Nevertheless, composers such as Hummel, Jan Ladislav Dusík (or Duschek, 1760–1812), and John Field (1782–1837), admired by Chopin and Schumann—and there are of course others—do not deserve to be completely forgotten. As to the construction, while the symphonic form as established for the new century by Viotti and Beethoven became the norm, the contours of the ripieno concerto are still discernible up to the middle of the nineteenth century; the first, second, and third solo portions of the opening sonata movement, each separated by the tutti of the orchestra, clearly hark back to the original Baroque form. The first solo comes after the initial half, or divided, exposition, not unlike the solo after the first ritornel of old; the second is the development section; the third the reprise; while the coda is usually left to the orchestra. At times the first tutti will not present the second or subsidiary theme, leaving it to be introduced by the soloist in his half of the exposition.

The basic esthetic problems of the concerto became painfully evident throughout the nineteenth century, due mainly to the unequal distribution of the musical substance between solo and orchestra. Mozart, Beethoven, Brahms, and a few others wrote concertos for "violin [or piano] *and* orchestra," but a concerto by Paganini is for "violin *with* orchestra," which makes for considerable difference. This latter approach made the concerto into the most perishable among instrumental genres, because its virtuoso fretwork is time-bound and quickly succumbs to changing tastes. Innumerable concertos were composed, but only those survive that managed to combine virtuosity with solid musical fare not subject to changing fashions. Corelli, Vivaldi, Geminiani, and other excellent Baroque composers are again coming into their own, but once vastly admired masters of the concerto such as Bériot, Vieuxtemps, Anton Rubinstein, d'Albert, heard early in our century to tumultuous applause, are gone forever. Glazunov's violin concerto was within memory a most welcome staple, but today it is very seldom, if ever, heard outside of conservatory concerts, and in a few years it will be retired to a mute existence on the library shelves. It is for this reason that we must cherish the concertos that are immune to the passing of fashions, as are almost all the scores in this anthology. There are, fortunately, many more excellent works still awaiting rehabilitation, and the twentieth century has produced splendid new ones.

❃ ❃ ❃

Beethoven's first piano concerto, in B♭, today mislabeled as No. 2, belongs not only chronologically but spiritually to the last decade of the eighteenth century. Beethoven obviously started out from Mozart, and he is quite formal, yet the work could not be mistaken for anyone else's. Within the eighteenth-century limits we also find such harbingers of Romanticism as the demand "con gran espressione." The next concerto, called the First (C major, Op. 15), now using a full orchestra, opens with a conventional "first movement" symphonic subject; it is well developed though rather according to the book, and on the whole it is insignificant, at least when measured by Beethovenian standards. But the Largo is a great piece, and the finale shows the earthy humor that is so characteristic of its composer. Now, however, Beethoven stops being a pupil: the Third Concerto (C minor, Op. 37, 1800) was his first attempt at reconciling an ample symphonic plan with the concerto. The tone is earnest, the proportions of the sonata structure large, and the relationship of solo and orchestra is searchingly explored. He still cannot free himself from a full preliminary orchestral exposition, but this is no longer a ritornel in simple sonata form; it is an extensive symphonic opening. Beethoven was aware of Mozart's highly original evasions of the pitfalls attending the difficult formal task of tying the solo into the symphonic process, one of the most difficult spots being at the end of the first ritornel when the solo enters; and it is clear that Mozart's C minor Concerto was in his mind when he composed his in the same key. The solution here is quite satisfactory, though Beethoven, the arch-symphonist, is unwilling to start the solo non-thematically, as does Mozart. The solo starts out all over again with the main subject, but the development is skilfully divided between solo and orchestra. Very impressive, very Classical, and very Beethovenian is the relentless thematic manipulation of a little rhythmic figure from the end of the principal subject; the composer holds on to it all the way to the remarkable coda—even the timpani play it, solo— while at the same time the piano part is appropriately virtuosic. The second movement is a little more conventional; nevertheless, no one before Beethoven would have ventured to write a movement in E major in a composition whose main tonality is C minor. The finale, again modeled on Mozart's C minor Concerto, is also fine, though its organization does not attain Mozart's perfection.

Beethoven must have thought a great deal about the formal conflicts created by the symphony-*cum*-concerto, for in the following concerto, the Fourth (G major, Op. 58, 1806), he put all his awesome might to work, determined to force a solution. Without any doubt, this is his greatest concerto, and one of the greatest of all time. Now the relationship between solo and orchestra shows both complete interdependence and sharp opposition, reaching in the slow movement the most dramatic confrontation ever achieved in a concerto. Beethoven no longer uses the stock, ready-made subjects that were still present in his first concertos and symphonies; he now composes his themes. The piano begins, dreamily, all by itself, as if to announce its independence, and while there is a "regulation" orchestral exposition, the burden is now better distributed. The piano is not restricted to the customary display episodes but is an active participant in the symphonic process, though the concertante quality is nowhere neglected. This, one is inclined to think, was an ideal solution of the symphony-concerto dichotomy. In the second movement, long-dormant memories are awakened with Romantic passion. This is an utterly dramatic *scena* that would seem to have a hidden program, the orchestra pressing the solo piano for an answer to its imperious questions, the latter's ineffable pleading gradually mollifying the rough strings until they subside. This is the tone of the old Italian violin concerto composed by born dramatists, now raised to undreamed-of heights, though surely Beethoven, not the studious kind, had no knowledge of the old masters. Vivaldi was by then so completely forgotten that the Viennese probably did not even know that the great Italian had died, destitute, sixty-odd years before, and was buried in their city. Beethoven's only possible intermediary to this style would have been the fiery Carl Philipp Emanuel Bach, but whoever it might have been, he is dwarfed by this extraordinary piece that shook the Romantic world. The third movement is concerted music of the first water, requiring all the virtuosity the player can summon; the two adversaries, for such they are, engage in battle, yet the symphonic work is most imaginatively carried out.

The next concerto should be expected to clinch the victory, with Beethoven asserting himself as completely as he did in sonata, quartet, and symphony. Yet he seems to have hit a snag, as he was later to do in the other two great sonata genres, quartet and symphony. After the dark-hued Quartet in F minor, Op. 95, there ensued an unconscionably long pause before he returned to the quartet. And in the Ninth Symphony he added a chorus and soloists to what had been the epitome of pure, "abstract" instrumental music, thus seeming to abandon the very principles he had so stubbornly followed. But after a hiatus of ten years he returned to the string quartet in his last great works, and his sketches show that he intended to compose a purely instrumental tenth symphony. So in both instances he recovered his bearings and went forward to new conquests. In the concerto, on the contrary, he fell back on a type that he had already mastered in the preceding Fourth Piano Concerto, and after this attempt gave up the genre, never to return to it.

The Fifth Concerto (E♭ major, Op. 73, 1809), his last, is perhaps a throwback, but what a throwback it is! Filled with proud, martial clangor, granting the soloist's virtuosity free rein, this concerto, which is Beethoven's *Eroica* among concertos, became, under the name of *Emperor Concerto,* his most popular work of its kind. The first movement, an enormous symphonic structure that is larger than the corresponding movement in the Ninth Symphony, starts out with improvisatory cadenzas by the piano, as if to embark on a far more adventurous treatment of the concerto-symphony than was the case in the G major Concerto; but after the initial roulades it settles down to a "normal" symphonic exposition, so fascinatingly elaborate that we forget that the piano is in the picture at all. Mozart does this too, in his D minor Concerto, among others, where the entry of the solo is so surprising that it takes a moment or two to realize that this is, after all, a concerto; after starting the solo with a thematically unrelated statement, he then craftily leads the listener back to the mainstream of the symphonic procedure. Beethoven here takes a leaf out of Mozart's book by starting the solo with a chromatic run, but immediately afterwards he resumes seamless thematic work. The development is magnificent, and the true concerto triumphs as Beethoven, now having at his disposal a robust instrument, pits its power against the full weight of the orchestra in a trial of strength never before seen in the concerto. The march-like, military character of this movement is dramatically exploited as Beethoven increasingly explores the extreme reaches of the piano, making the solo play the march ethereally in the highest register. The recapitulation is literal, including even the first improvisatory runs, though Beethoven incorporates a written-out cadenza of his own before ending with a mighty coda. The second is a deeply felt hymnic movement. Beethoven once more makes the piano diffuse heavenly figurations while the orchestra sings a prayer; then, with a stroke of genius, he suddenly drops the tonality by half a tone and a hush descends upon everything. This movement is in the key of B major—unusual considering the main tonality, E♭ major—and one would think that an elaborate modulation is in order to usher in the beginning of the third movement, which follows without pause. By simply dropping from B to B♭, we are instantly on the dominant of the principal key, and Beethoven delicately prepares us for what is to come. But when the finale sets in, all restraint is thrown to the winds; orchestra and soloist burst out with the kind of boundless jubilation that recalls Florestan's and Leonore's ecstatic duet in *Fidelio* —there is even a certain kinship in the themes. This is the virtuoso concerto in the grand manner, carried out with the most ingenious and varied symphonic development, with endless combinations and permutations of the melodically and metrically intricate ideas. We must conclude that Beethoven had abandoned the idea of a complete symphonic integration so auspiciously begun in the G major Concerto, composing instead a superb concerto that is perhaps "old-fashioned" in concept but overwhelmingly magnificent in execution and brimming with original ideas.

✻ ✻ ✻

The first movement of Beethoven's Violin Concerto (D major, Op. 61, 1806) surprises with its multiplicity of ideas, yet it is dominated in true symphonic fashion by one of these, an extraordinary one indeed: the concerto begins with a kettledrum solo! The five notes of this theme —it is once more the "military" theme of the French violin concerto— are presented in startling variety by the simple expedient of keeping the rhythmic pattern but changing the melodic interval between the fourth and fifth notes, in turn enabling the composer constantly to surprise us with the harmony. Remarkable also is the passage work, for Beethoven is never satisfied with mere virtuoso heroics; there is always melodic substance in the solo violin's ruminations. There are some profundly moving episodes, like the one in G minor in the middle of the movement, and the return of the violin after the cadenza. The symphonic construction is tight, the introductory five-note motif not only ever-present but, in Beethoven's unique way, at times insistent; yet the soloist's freedom is not curtailed. At the approach of the recapitulation the symphonic intensity becomes very strong, and the reprise starts with powerful iterations of the five-note motif by an aroused orchestra. The second movement, again on the French model, is a "romance," a type that Beethoven had used previously as an independent piece (Opp. 40 and 50). It is lyrical to a markedly Romantic degree. As the orchestra begins the movement, the muted strings sing a beautiful melody out of which rise the sublime garlands of the solo violin. Nothing here but peace and ravishing sound, though the harmonies are gently surprising. A brief cadenza leads over to the finale, a sonata-rondo of a sweepingly virtuoso nature. This is a "hunt" piece, the *chasse* of the French concerto; the horns bugle and even the violins hop and skip in angular intervals. Very attractive is the little hesitation that precedes the return of the rondo theme.

This, like the last two piano concertos, is a great work; it will live as long as violins are played and orchestras are maintained. Yet, as we look at the chronological sequence of the concertos, we cannot help seeing that Beethoven was experiencing a certain limitation of his creative freedom. Both Mozart and Beethoven were virtuoso performers and they composed for virtuosos, yet both faithfully guarded the composer's integrity. Mozart, still entirely under the eighteenth-century concept of social entertainment music, did not question the purpose of the concerto, nor did he worry about the esthetic and formal problems caused by the merging of the Baroque concerto with the Classical symphony. His inexhaustible imagination took everything in its stride, and he always found the solution needed for any particular situation. These solutions were, however, highly personal and inimitable, and therefore did not contribute to the ultimate settlement of the problems inherent in the species. Beethoven, though no longer bound by the same social purpose, nevertheless could not entirely throw off the restrictions created by the compromise form. He was not the flexible dramatist that Mozart was, used to ever-changing conflicts; his grand symphonic imagination needed less equivocal boundaries for the full exertion of his powers. The pathbreaking Third Symphony (the *Eroica*) and the tremendous *Sonata Appassionata* preceded the G major Piano Concerto; the Violin Concerto was composed in 1806, while Beethoven was working on the Fifth and Sixth Symphonies and the great Third *Leonore* Overture; the *Emperor Concerto* following in 1809. While these three concertos are justly admired and immortal works, they do not quite reach the exceptional plateau occupied by Beethoven's other works corresponding to them in time. We shall see that other composers, especially Brahms, were similarly inconvenienced by inherited limitations.

❊ ❊ ❊

Mendelssohn, in many ways a traditionalist, nevertheless must be credited with one of the most original solutions of the concerto *versus* symphony problem. In his Violin Concerto (E minor, Op. 64, 1844) there is no introductory exposition; the violin starts right at the beginning, and not with the usual virtuoso preamble but with the principal theme, which is then neatly developed in close cooperation with the orchestra. The interplay, masterful and very attractive, is full of the most ingenious and hitherto unheard-of combinations of solo with orchestra. There is, for instance, the magic spot where the solo descends to the lowest tone of the instrument, holding it as a pedal point, while above it the wood-winds play a fine melody. Masterful also is the cadenza, composed in its entirety by Mendelssohn, insuring an ideal and stylistic unity that is never achieved when the cadenza is composed by someone else. The second movement is a "song without words" in concerto form, a warm cantilena for the violin, though in the middle it strikes a passionate tone. The finale recaptures the scintillating fairy world of the *Midsummer Night's Dream* music; it flits and bounds in an animated sonata-rondo, and though virtuosic in the extreme, the symphonic work is outstanding. The delectable glitter is leavened by a quiet melody that affords just the right contrast. This is a sunny, beguiling work of eternal freshness that remains poetic even in the whirlwind finale.

❖ ❖ ❖

Carl Maria von Weber is best known for his opera *Der Freischütz*, and several of his accomplished overtures used to be popular in orchestral concerts. But he was also an excellent pianist who should not be omitted from the gallery of early Romantic composers for the piano. Of his concertos, only the *Konzertstück* (F minor, Op. 79, 1821) is still regularly heard, though his E♭ major Concerto should be reactivated, for it has one of the most beautiful slow movements in the entire Romantic piano literature. Weber was a man of the theater, born and raised on the boards, and whatever he composed had a dramatic touch to it. A century before, the early Italian concerto already had little dramatic scenes, and the slow movement in Beethoven's G major Piano Concerto is a true dramatic *scena*, even though not so named. Now the early Romantic composers, anticipating the developments in Paris during the Meyer-beerian era, write one-movement concertos in a decidedly operatic vein. Ludwig Spohr's violin concerto "in the form of a vocal *scena*" (1816), an outstanding example of the species, is still played occasionally, and deservedly saved from oblivion. Weber's *Konzertstück* is its counter-part in the piano concerto. This "Concert Piece" has a program, a typically Romantic program about the châtelaine pining for her knight away on a crusade. But we should not worry about the sentimental story; the dramatic apparatus, especially the recitative, makes excellent musical sense in purely instrumental terms. The *Konzertstück* offers gratifying entertainment.

❖ ❖ ❖

Robert Schumann, the composer of our next concerto, invites particular attention and praise for his sole work in the genre for his own instrument. He was a pianist, his bride was an acknowledged virtuoso, and as a critic he became familiar with a large part of the concerto literature; one would naturally expect him to compose in this popular genre. Still, for some time he refused to undertake the composition of a concerto even for Clara. Though a man of considerable culture, Schumann was not given to theoretical speculation, nor did he have a historical sense or appreciation, and aside from Bach, Mozart, Beethoven, Schubert, and a little Haydn and Handel, he did not know music older than that of his own generation. It was only relatively late in life that he began to study old music. His music criticism was more a form of engaging Romantic literary fantasy than workmanlike analysis, and it is unlikely that he was aware of the specific problems of the concerto that made Beethoven abandon the genre. What deterred him from the concerto was his loathing of the virtuoso who wants a show at the expense of the composition—and most of the contemporary concertos he heard *ex officio* were in that category. We must also realize that members of his generation, with the exception of Mendelssohn, were temperamentally and instinctively alienated from the architectural sonata form, and the sonata-concerto only exacerbated their difficulties. But Schumann did hit upon a solution, composing, in 1840, a Fantasy in A minor for Piano and Orchestra. And an original and successful solution it was: a dialogue piece which, while observing the general contours of the sonata, avoids all the dual features of the old concerto. There are no real ritornels, few sharp confrontations of contending forces; the solo instrument is in the center and remains there throughout the piece. The thematic material—most appealing—is developed in a dialogue between the two partners, and stimulating exchanges are provided for solo woodwinds and the piano. The thematic elaboration, in highly idiomatic pianistic terms, is remarkable for a Romantic composer whose every instinct rebelled against logic and consequence. The cadenza, written out completely by the composer, as in Mendessohn's Violin Concerto, is a little masterpiece in itself, and is beautifully timed. Five years later, Schumann rounded out the Fantasy to a full-fledged concerto by adding two other movements. The delectable dialogue is carried further in the second movement, but in a refined, intimate fashion that was altogether new in the concerto; here indeed was the victory over the virtuoso that Schumann dreamed about. The finale, a proud movement, full of élan and palpably influenced by the finale of the *Emperor Concerto*, shows cyclic connections with the first movement, expressed in interesting rhythmic patterns. Here the spirit of the concerto is fully present, including dramatic confrontations between piano and orchestra, but always on Schumann's terms. The spacious sonata structure of this movement did inconvenience Schumann; he repeats the exposition literally, and in the large coda he is constrained (as in his symphonies) to introduce a beautiful new melody to tide him over the slackening symphonic process—but the élan holds, and the music still sparkles. This concerto remains one of the finest of the species, and a good conductor will know how to deal with the awkward spots in the orchestration, which was not one of Schumann's strong points.

❆ ❆ ❆

The concerto takes a new turn under the influence of the Parisian school, international in membership but united under the aegis of French taste and the dramatic effects of the rising grand opera. Over-wrought pathos alternating with empty virtuosity, loose construction, and shallow musical ideas are the characteristic marks of this new concerto. But the ostentatiously grateful solo parts were loved by both players and public, though the leading critics, Berlioz and Schumann, sneered at them, belaboring their composers with unsparing scorn. The compositions became so one-sided that in many instances the orchestra could simply be omitted or, in the case of violin concertos, replaced by a piano. With one exception, we need not be concerned with this trend in Paris until we reach Liszt; but the one great composer caught in the showmen's game calls for attention. While Chopin's concertos are flawed, they nevertheless rise far above the soulless exhibitionism of the Parisian coterie of pianists.

Chopin's name stands for the most original invention, marvelous pianistic sense, and highly personal harmonic ideas; Schumann called him "a cannon buried in flowers." Yet all these gifts did not suffice to cope with the concerto. To Chopin the large and elaborate form of the sonata was alien—his piano sonatas consist of strings of fine pieces joined into sets—so when he decided on the composition of a concerto, he simply followed the model established by the new Parisian virtuoso school. The F minor Concerto (Op. 21, 1829) is in fact a conventional virtuoso concerto, indifferent in construction and poor in the handling of the orchestra. Chopin uses what remains of the once-substantial ritornels, but there is no conviction in their shaping; he wants to get at the piano as quickly as possible. The solo part reverts to the old display episodes as Chopin, a great admirer of Hummel, follows the latter's highly ornate writing in etude style but without Hummel's ability to coordinate these garlands with the rest of the composition; the piano part is largely by itself. But—and it is a large but—the great poet of the piano is still there, as is the most original pianistic imagination, which never fails to fascinate. The form may be awkward, the orchestra a bit hapless, the sutures quite obvious, but this music can still move the heartstrings, and no work by any member of the musical colony in Paris could hold a candle to it. The second movement is a ravishing "nocturne" (though not so called) which is perhaps a little overloaded with fiorituras, but it sings and it musters eloquence. The finale is again in the conventional virtuoso manner, though if well played it is not without charm. Both of Chopin's concertos have been repeatedly—and necessarily—reorchestrated (abbreviating the tuttis, which is often done, is no solution); it is high time, however, for some knowledgeable and respectful musician to undertake this task and deliver Chopin from the pedagogues and the Kapellmeisters. An amusing example of the questionable assistance rendered to Chopiin is Balakirev's reorchestration of the E minor Concerto —one amateur symphonist helping another!

✻   ✻   ✻

The French themselves tired of the impoverished concerto, and a movement began to rehabilitate the orchestra and seek a new synthesis. The originators of the movement are today forgotten, but the man who really carried it to fruition, Franz Liszt, is not, even though he was and still is the subject of the most violently contradictory appraisals. Liszt dedicated his E♭ major Concerto to Henry Litolff (1818–1891), in recognition of an artistic debt to the man whose concertos gave him the incentive for his own contributions; Liszt may have been vain and bombastic, but he was always generous toward his fellow musicians. Litolff, a pianist born in England but at home in Paris, was a kindred soul both as man and artist. He roamed the world, dazzled audiences with his playing, and composed some concertos remarkable for their novel ideas, brilliance of orchestration, and originality of construction. Nevertheless, it was Liszt who brought about a really modern regeneration of the ailing concerto, even though his two such works represent the virtuoso concerto *in excelsis*. Everything we found negative in Chopin is in the E♭ Concerto present in triumphantly positive shape; the form is splendidly original, the bravura far exceeds Chopin's and Hummel's elegant reticence, being the most extrovert, explosive kind imaginable. The orchestration is superb, the sound invigorating, and over the whole there hovers a personality of overwhelming force. Liszt presents a unique case. His ideas are usually mediocre and often banal, but his sense of utilization of what he had to say was phenomenal. He played the piano as Paganini played the violin, with an irresistible personal involvement that projected like the beam of a searchlight. "Histrionic epilepsy" was Heine's term for the effect Liszt's playing exerted on the audience, and somehow he managed to get this quality into the music itself. His ideas may be commonplace, but their execution is seductive. Many musicians despised him, then and now, for this very reason, but few could escape his lure. Liszt's pianism, especially his sonic imagination, created a school altogether different from Chopin's, for the piano is now as formidable as the orchestra and has as many colors.

The E♭ Concerto (1848, subsequently revised) offers a concept that was altogether new and remains original to this day. It is a multi-movement plan telescoped into one, and while it is possible to distinguish the individual components, they are convincingly integrated into one large unit, markedly cyclic in nature. The rhythms are sharp, the principal theme, if conventional, is terse and eminently suited for manipulation. The piano is off, in full cry, by the fifth measure, and nothing could stop its all-embracing virtuosity, yet Liszt skilfully varies the stormy texture with soft Romantic melodies that make the contrast more effective. The slow movement emerges quite naturally as a sort of extended episode, and Liszt calls on the whole arsenal of Romantic devices: the melting cello melody, the dramatic recitative, and so forth. Everything is eclectic and yet somehow utterly personal. Then comes a scherzo section, swift, piquant, and superbly orchestrated, leading to a finale that makes use of previous thematic material in imaginative ways as the concerto ends in a blazing tangle of piano and orchestra. Liszt shocked the critics and the first audiences by the use of the triangle. This is, of course, the old story; no one before had thought of it, so when the first composer to make use of the triangle in a concerto comes along, he is condemned.

Liszt was born in Hungary, went early to live in Paris, and became the resident sage in Weimar. Each of these three countries claims him, but he was an international artist, and if the spirit of any of the claimant countries was close to his heart, it was that of French Romanticism.

❖ ❖ ❖

Liszt's bold innovation had no immediate sequel; his daring originality was still strong meat, especially for the composers of the symphonic heartland, Germany. Interestingly enough, it was the most conservative member of this conservative heartland who created the outstanding concertos of the late Romantic era.

Brahms started out greatly inconvenienced by the old formal problems of the concerto; his First Piano Concerto (D minor, Op. 15, 1858) was not born, it was manipulated into being. First conceived as a symphony, it was then reworked into a sonata for two pianos. The composer was still not satisfied—Beethoven's scepter forced him to severe self-criticism—but since the transformation gave the work a pianistic flavor,

Brahms now decided on a third version, which became his First Concerto. And a peculiar piece it is, the greatest contrast imaginable to Liszt's avant-garde concept of a decade earlier. The virtuoso element is, in Schumann's spirit, minimized, though the solo part is very difficult because of Brahm's somewhat ungainly piano writing that keeps all ten fingers busy at all times. The orchestration is also dense, obviously causing Brahms difficulties. This texture is like a too-closely-planted flower garden. Nevertheless, the work abounds in beauties that none of Brahms's contemporaries could summon, and it is decidedly to be counted among the great concertos.

The Second Piano Concerto, composed a quarter of a century later (B♭ major, Op. 83, 1881), is quite another work. Aside from the experience gained during the intervening years, Brahms spent a couple of seasons in Italy, and one cannot help seeing a certain southern warmth and clarity invading the music of the stern North German master. But then by this time Brahms was a Viennese by adoption, and the spirit of the Mediterranean had always been particularly congenial to the Viennese; without it the great Classical school we call "Viennese" would never have arisen. The D minor Concerto is dark and tragic, echoing, it is said, the grief and shock caused by Schumann's death, but the B♭ Concerto is friendly and warm. It is a large work, and Brahms keeps it within the traditional concerto-sonata frame, with discernible separation of the ritornels, the piano usually beginning its part with a little cadenza-like entry, which, as we have seen, was Mozart's innovation. (Brahms was a real connoisseur of music and its history, probably the best-informed musician of his time, and whenever we see some archaic trait in his compositions we can be sure this is the result not of fortuitous circumstances but of serious study.) While the formal plan of this concerto does not take notice of newer concepts, tone and substance do: this is a full-blooded Romantic concerto, with dreamy horn calls and broadly flowing melodies, offset by the prickly rhythm of the subsidiary themes. Also, while there is a "second tutti," as the book demands, it is in F minor, a tonal relationship decidedly not in the book. The thematic work is outstanding, free from Brahms's sometimes labored ways, and there is a comradely understanding between solo and orchestra. There was one thing that Brahms did accept from the modern Parisian school: the four-movement form with scherzo. The second movement in this concerto is such a scherzo, and an elaborate, swift, beautifully constructed, true symphonic scherzo it is. All nineteenth-century composers (with the exception of Schubert) experienced difficulties with the symphonic scherzo because their path was blocked by the formidable and inimitable

Beethovenian model. By the time of this concerto, Brahms had composed two symphonies, neither of which had a scherzo; now, no longer inhibited, he reveled in his freedom from the oppressive shadow, even venturing onto Beethoven's own ground—for this scherzo does not simply romp, it is dusky, and the symphonic proportions are those of a major movement. The third movement quickly disperses the clouds; everything sings here, especially the "Romantic" instruments—cello, horn, and clarinet—while the piano accompanies with un-Brahmsian airiness. The fine movement actually quotes two Brahms songs, *Todessehnen* and *Immer leiser*. The finale is a virtuoso piece in the spirit of the old concerto, the usual rondo-like construction with a remarkable variety in the metamorphoses of the refrain. Here there is rivalry in the true spirit of the concerto, but nowhere does Brahms make concessions at the expense of a well-composed, spirited movement.

* * *

Brahms's only violin concerto (D major, Op. 77, 1878) also follows the Classical plan. The technical requirements are considerable, yet the work is not really a virtuoso concerto, even though the solo part was enlivened under the guidance of Joseph Joachim, the leading German violinist of the day. One immediately feels that Beethoven's Violin Concerto stood as godfather at the birth of this grand composition, and the nobility of the model is well reflected in the younger master's work. The construction of the first movement is perhaps a little too conventionally traditional—the reprise is literal—but the principal themes are thoughtfully separated by a sharply rhythmical subsidiary theme which always appears at the right spot at the right time. Brahms takes a leaf out of Beethoven's score in the way he reintroduces the principal theme after the cadenza, but does it magnificently. The slow movement is Brahmsian to its fingertips, a deeply felt song of great melodic beauty, in which the solo oboe and the solo violin share the honors. Brahms unfolds this melody with quiet but fervent enthusiasm, and when the solo violin climbs high above the orchestra, the music becomes incandescent. The closing movement, a rousing, pointedly rhythmic and zestful piece, shows that Brahms had become acclimatized to the Austrian capital. The principal theme, treated in rondo fashion, is one of those half-Eastern-, half–Western-European tunes that only Vienna, with its amalgam of German, Hungarian, Slavic, and Gypsy music, could produce. Brahms coaxed a remarkable variety of configurations out of it.

Surprisingly, given the quality of the two concertos discussed here, the old insecurity about the concerto-symphony flairs up in all its intensity in Brahms's Double Concerto for Violin and Cello (A minor,

Op. 102, 1887). Perhaps the reason was that the material utilized in this hybrid work was originally destined for a fifth symphony. The concerto has many fine points, but on the whole it bears the marks of this indecision, and, as someone has said, the two solo instruments are often handled like "an eight-stringed giant fiddle."

* * *

The concerto, which was an Italian "invention" and which produced so many masterpieces in eighteenth-century Italy, all but disappeared in the land of its origin in the nineteenth. The one celebrity, Paganini, who composed violin concertos of diabolical difficulty but poor artistic quality, really belongs to the French school. In other countries beyond the main Austro-German arena, many concertos were composed during the last century, some of which—those of Grieg, MacDowell, and Saint-Saëns come to mind—are still heard, even if infrequently. But even the latter are period pieces that are rapidly losing their ties to our world. Only one among these peripheral composers of concertos was able to rival the Western masters: Tchaikovsky, whose B♭ minor Piano Concerto (Op. 23, 1875) and D major Violin Concerto (Op. 35, 1878) became the most widely heard and acclaimed works of this genre originating in the second half of the nineteenth century. The secret of this enormous and lasting success rests on the combination of sweepingly brilliant writing for the solo instrument with melting, long-grained, ultra-Romantic melodies, and with popular Russian tunes, all of it skillfully kept in the clear—nothing is ever covered or obscured here—and the whole wrapped in a lively and colorful orchestral garb. The B♭ minor Concerto has had a devastating effect on concertgoers, and while the reaction to Romantic excesses has trimmed this popularity somewhat, the concerto is still the trump card of the virtuoso. No pianist can consider himself *arrivé* until he can launch successfully into the crashing chords, the racing octaves, and the bracing runs of this world-conquering concerto. Perhaps we are tired of this kind of overheated music, of its banalities, and occasional grossness, but there can be no question about Tchaikovsky's gifts, his exceptional sense for aural effectiveness, his mastery of the orchestra as well as of the piano, his unerring ear for what sounds well. Nor can we deny that in this particular concerto he combined all these so well that he created a sort of landmark in the history of the concerto. Hanslick, the famous critic, called this concerto "dirty music," and many people share his view; they are not only uncharitable but wrong. Tchaikovsky does take the easy way out by repeating instead of developing, each repetition getting more hysterical than the previous one, and he can be sentimental, arch, and very noisy, but this is a genuine, if slightly tawdry, virtuoso concerto that has proved its staying power for almost a century.

❖ ❖ ❖

Among instruments other than the piano and the violin, only the cello interested the composers of concertos in the latter part of the nineteenth century. The cello concerto has a distinguished ancestry; there are some fine old compositions by the Viennese Georg Matthias Monn, Haydn, Emanuel Bach, and Boccherini, but there are few from the nineteenth century deserving notice. This is understandable. There were, of course, composing cello virtuosos, but few, if any, showed creative originality. On the other hand, the great composers were handicapped by difficulties the instrument presented when used with orchestra. The most attractive timbre of the cello is in the bass-tenor region, which it occupies naturally by virtue of its tonal position in the violin family. If it stays in its natural habitat for any length of time, however, it will fail to hold the listener's attention, even though the warm cello tone rivals that of the French horn in romantic appeal. When ascending to the treble region, the warmth easily turns into a nasal, even pinched tone quality, the intonation becomes critical and hazardous, and only the exceptional player can safely cope with it. It takes very good playing, indeed, to minimize, reconcile, and blend the two extremes. And of course in the Romantic era there was the danger of banking too much on the expressive qualities of the typical cello register. (This was also true of the G string of the violin, which in the Romantic concerto was exploited to a degree to make the stones weep.) The cello concertos of the nineteenth century are full of soulful romanzas, pathetic recitatives, and growling bass passages, which made them hopelessly dated within one generation. No wonder all that remains from this nineteenth-century concerto literature is one work by Schumann, one (No. 2) by Saint-Saëns, and one by Dvořák, the latter by far the finest of the lot. Composed during Dvořák's stay in the United States around 1894–95, it is distinguished by a remarkable sense for favoring the solo part idiomatically without neglecting the symphonic work. Most felicitous is the orchestration, which, by its contrasting effects, makes the cello stand out without effort. The aural qualities of this concerto are exceptionally pleasing, and the ideas developed are very attractive. In this late work Dvořák shows a certain eclecticism: Brahms and Schubert rub elbows with Tchaikovsky, the exquisite slow movement is palpably patterned after Brahms's Violin Concerto, the ritornel being played by the winds alone, as in the model. But somehow Dvořák always comes out on top and remains his Czech self.

* * *

The twentieth century once more reorganized the concerto according to its own lights, and a valuable literature is gradually replacing all but the timeless masterpieces. The concertos printed in this anthology will live, and many more by the old masters will join them, but certain antiquated and objectionable practices will have to be eliminated before these older masters will shine again in their full glory. One of these malpractices, playing Bach or Mozart with a full Straussian orchestra, is now happily becoming a thing of the past. The original small orchestra, in which the few wind instruments—as well as the soloist—are not drowned by a torrent of strings, is back in favor, and we can enjoy the delicate interplay of solo and orchestra in an eighteenth-century concerto. But one glaring anachronism still disfigures these works: the modern cadenza.

The orchestra is assembled, the conductor on his stand; then there emerges from the wings the great pianist, greeted with thunderous applause. He sits down and goes through the ritual that precedes the concerto. First he works the hoisting mechanism of his seat: up and down, up again and down again, until he ends where he originally started from. Then he stretches his legs to feel the pedals, tries out his reach to the keyboard, wrings his hands a couple of times, finally beckoning to the conductor, who raises his baton, and the somber strains of, say, Mozart's D minor concerto begin in the orchestra. During the introduction the soloist still fidgets a little, but soon his turn comes, and he is happily occupied.

Eventually, the first movement draws toward its close, when suddenly the orchestra begins to slow down until it reaches a six-four chord upon which to settle, holding it, at the conductor's urgent behest, until there is hardly a whiff of air left in the wind players' lungs; when that point is reached, everyone stops. Violins are lowered into their players' laps, the bass fiddlers relax their grip on the giants of the orchestra, the brasses open the little spigots on their instruments to let the accumulated saliva drip into little pools, the timpanist drops his sticks, and the conductor tries to assume the air of an interested onlooker. For the next ten minutes or so they have nothing to do—neither does the composer—for the soloist takes over all by himself: he is playing the cadenza. At first everything is tame and orderly, as the listener recognizes snatches of the main theme of the movement, but soon the fireworks start, the performer racing over the keyboard with an enthusiastic abandon heretofore absent from his playing. The harmonies become fancier and fancier—Mozart would not have dreamed of such lushness—and every trace of the original mood of the work vanishes. Just when we begin to wonder what has happened to the concerto, the distinguished virtuoso begins to play trills, whereupon the violins are unlimbered, the bass fiddles are firmly seized, fists are stuffed into the bells of the dried-out horns, the timpanist picks up his mallets, and the conductor raises his baton, somewhat tentatively, watching the soloist from the corner of his eye. There is a final trill, and by a gentlemen's agreement, sealed with a mutual nod, the orchestra falls in, more or less at the same time that the soloist finally surrenders.

The idea of the cadenza itself, to heighten the denouement by delaying it, is an old and proven device, but often today's cadenza is a musical horror if not blatant exhibitionism. In the eighteenth century and in Beethoven's time, the cadenza was improvised on the spur of the moment and played by the composer himself, but with the appearance of the concertizing virtuoso, not himself a composer, the situation became awkward; the hiatus between the six-four chord and the last trill had to be filled out by someone other than the composer. Gradually the cadenzas, devised by part-time composers, developed into virtually independent pieces having only tenuous connections with the original movements, and became longer and longer. They are mostly worthless, and indeed are doomed before they start, because by the time a Beethoven or a Brahms arrives at the six-four chord the thematic material has been developed to the maximum extent; what could a lesser mind add to it? Beethoven was already suspicious of the cadenza makers, and besides incorporating a brief cadenza of his own into the *Emperor Concerto,* he expressly warned the soloist: "Do not make a cadenza here." Mendelssohn, with his fine sense of form, realized that a lengthy cadenza at the very end of a developed symphonic movement virtually negates the formal plan; he therefore placed the cadenza—his own—in the middle of the first movement of his Violin Concerto, a unique and most satisfactory way of dealing with this dangerous appendix to the concerto. It is high time that all posthumous cadenzas foisted on the works of the Classical masters be abolished. Since it is jarring to insert into a concerto a cadenza whose language is far removed from the composer's, and since it is unreasonable to expect a good present-day composer to furnish a period piece, the only solution is to dispense with the cadenza. If a cadenza by the original composer is available (both Mozart and Beethoven wrote them), it should be used, though without being prettied up or extended. If it is not available, a few tasteful runs after the six-four chord would take care of the suspended animation caused by the stop, but the integrity and continuity of the work would be saved and Reinecke, Joachim, Kreisler, and all the others relieved of the staggering responsibility of helping Mozart or Beethoven round out their concertos.

THE CONCERTO

1800–1900

A Norton Music Anthology

Ludwig van Beethoven (1770–1827)

CONCERTO FOR VIOLIN AND ORCHESTRA
IN D MAJOR, OP. 61

(1806)

INSTRUMENTATION

Flute (*Fl.*)
2 Oboes (*Ob.*)
2 Clarinets (*Clar.*) in A, C
2 Bassoons (*Fag.*)

2 Horns (*Cor.*) in D, G
2 Trumpets (*Trombe*) in D
Timpani (*Timp.*) in D, A

Solo Violin (*Viol. principale*)

Violin I
Violin II
Viola
Cello (*Vcl.*)
Bass (*Basso*)

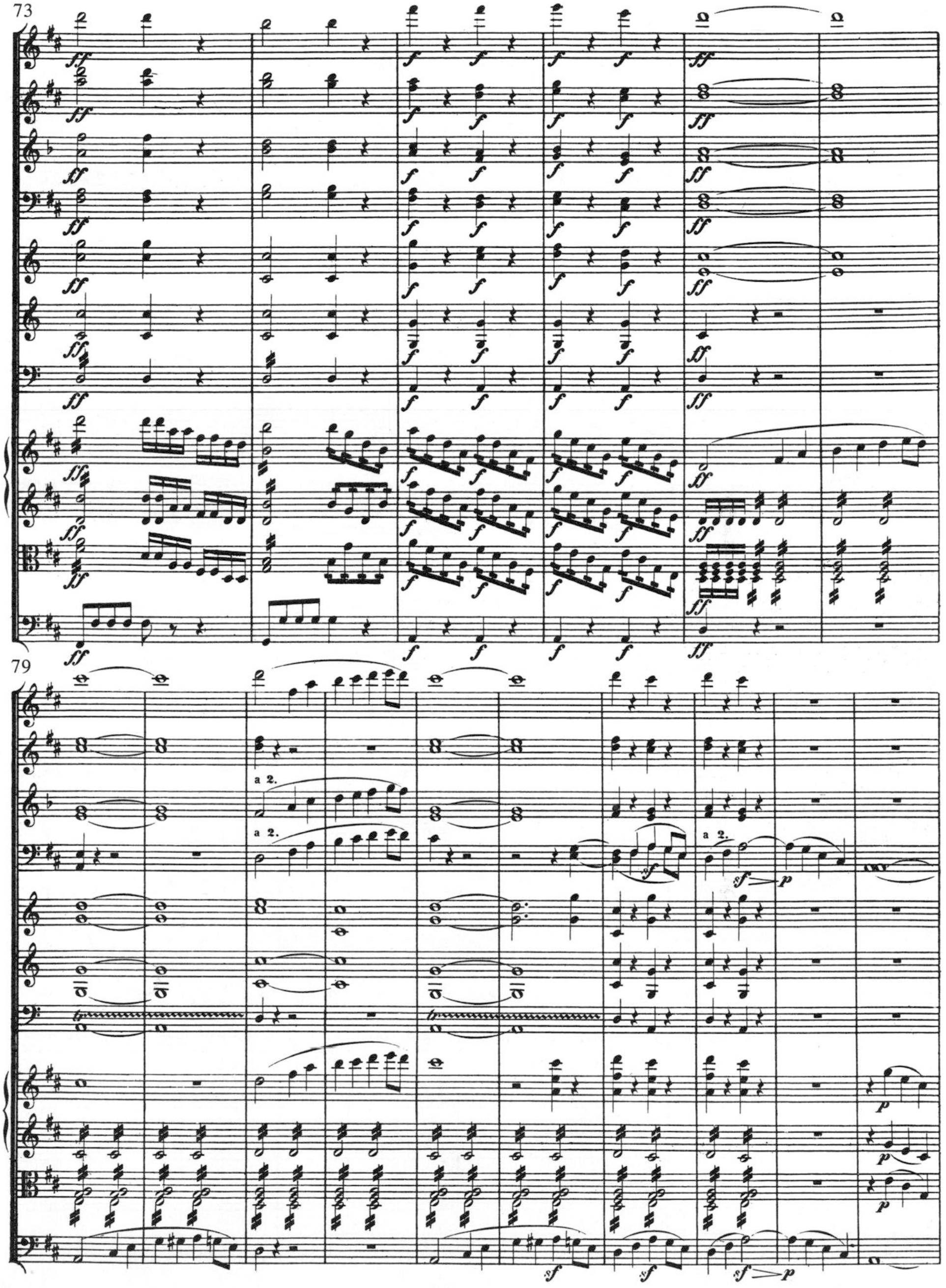
73
79
a 2.
a 2.
a 2.

17
Fl.
TUTTI
Ob.
Clar.
Fag.
Cor.
Trombe
Timp.
ten.
tr
ff
p
p Vel.
unis.
26
a2
sf

Ludwig van Beethoven

CONCERTO NO. 5 FOR PIANO AND ORCHESTRA
IN Eb MAJOR, OP. 73

(1 8 0 9)

INSTRUMENTATION

2 Flutes *(Fl.)*
2 Oboes *(Ob.)*
2 Clarinets *(Clar.)* in Bb *(B)*, A
2 Bassoons *(Fag.)*

2 Horns *(Cor.)* in Eb *(Es)*, D
2 Trumpets *(Tr.)* in Eb *(Es)*
Timpani *(Timp.)* in Eb, Bb

Solo Piano *(Pfte.)*

Violin I *(Viol. I)*
Violin II *(Viol. II)*
Viola
Cello *(Vcllo.)*
Bass *(C.-B.)*

NB. Non si fa una Cadenza, ma s'attacca subito il seguente

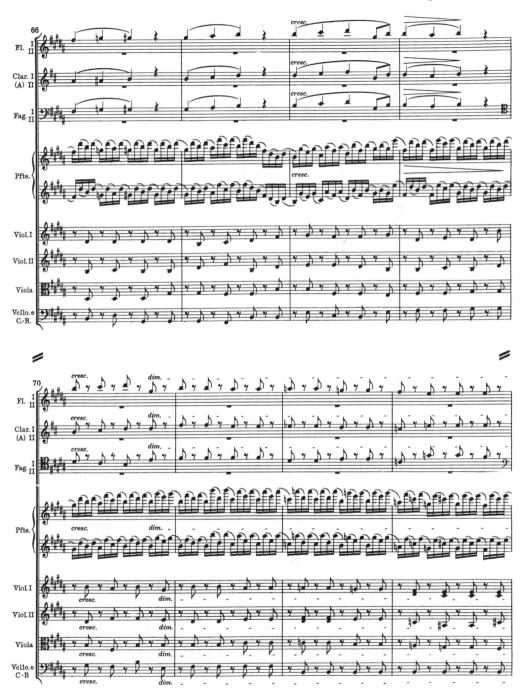

NB. Semplice poco tenuto

Carl Maria von Weber *(1786–1826)*

KONZERTSTÜCK FOR PIANO AND ORCHESTRA
IN F MINOR, OP. 79

(1 8 2 1)

INSTRUMENTATION

2 Flutes (*Fl.*)
2 Oboes (*Ob.*)
2 Clarinets (*Cl.*) in B♭
2 Bassoons (*Fag.*)

2 Horns (*Cor.*) in F, C
2 Trumpets (*Tr.*) in F, C
Bass Trombone (*Tromb.*)
Timpani (*Timp.*) in C, F, G

Solo Piano

Violin I
Violin II
Viola
Cello (*Violonc.*)
Bass (*Contra B., Basso*)

227 **Tempo di Marcia** (♩=126.)

Tempo di Marcia

234

Frédéric Chopin (1810–1849)

CONCERTO FOR PIANO AND ORCHESTRA
IN F MINOR, OP. 21

(1829)

INSTRUMENTATION

2 Flutes (*Fl.*)
2 Oboes (*Ob.*)
2 Clarinets (*Cl.*) in B♭
2 Bassoons (*Fag.*)

2 Horns (*Cor.*) in F, E♭ (*Es*)
2 Trumpets (*Trbe.*) in B♭ (*B*)
Bass Trombone (*Trb. Basso*)
Timpani (*Timp.*) in F, C

Solo Piano

Violin I
Violin II
Viola
Cello
Bass

498

Felix Mendelssohn (1809–1847)

CONCERTO FOR VIOLIN AND ORCHESTRA
IN E MINOR, OP. 64

(1844)

INSTRUMENTATION

2 Flutes
2 Oboes
2 Clarinets in A
2 Bassoons

2 Horns in E
2 Trumpets in E
Timpani in E, B

Solo Violin

Violin I
Violin II
Viola
Cello
Bass

61
a 2.
ff
a 2.
ff
a 2.
ff
sf
ff
sf
sf
ff
sf
ff
sf
sf
ff
sf
ff
sf
69
C
p
a 2.
p
fp
fp
p
ff
ff
p
p
C
p
p

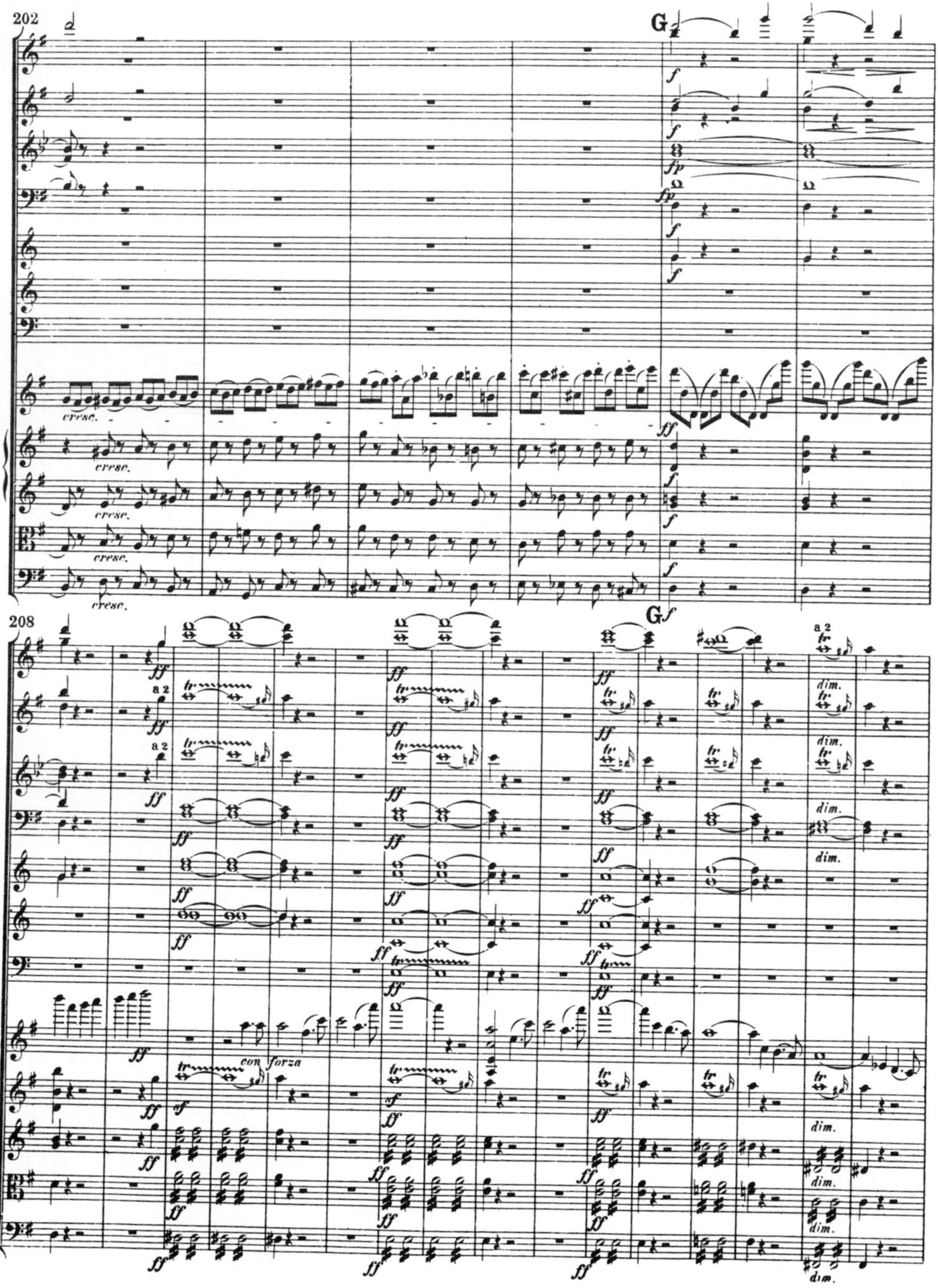
202
G
cresc.
208
G
a 2
con forza
dim.

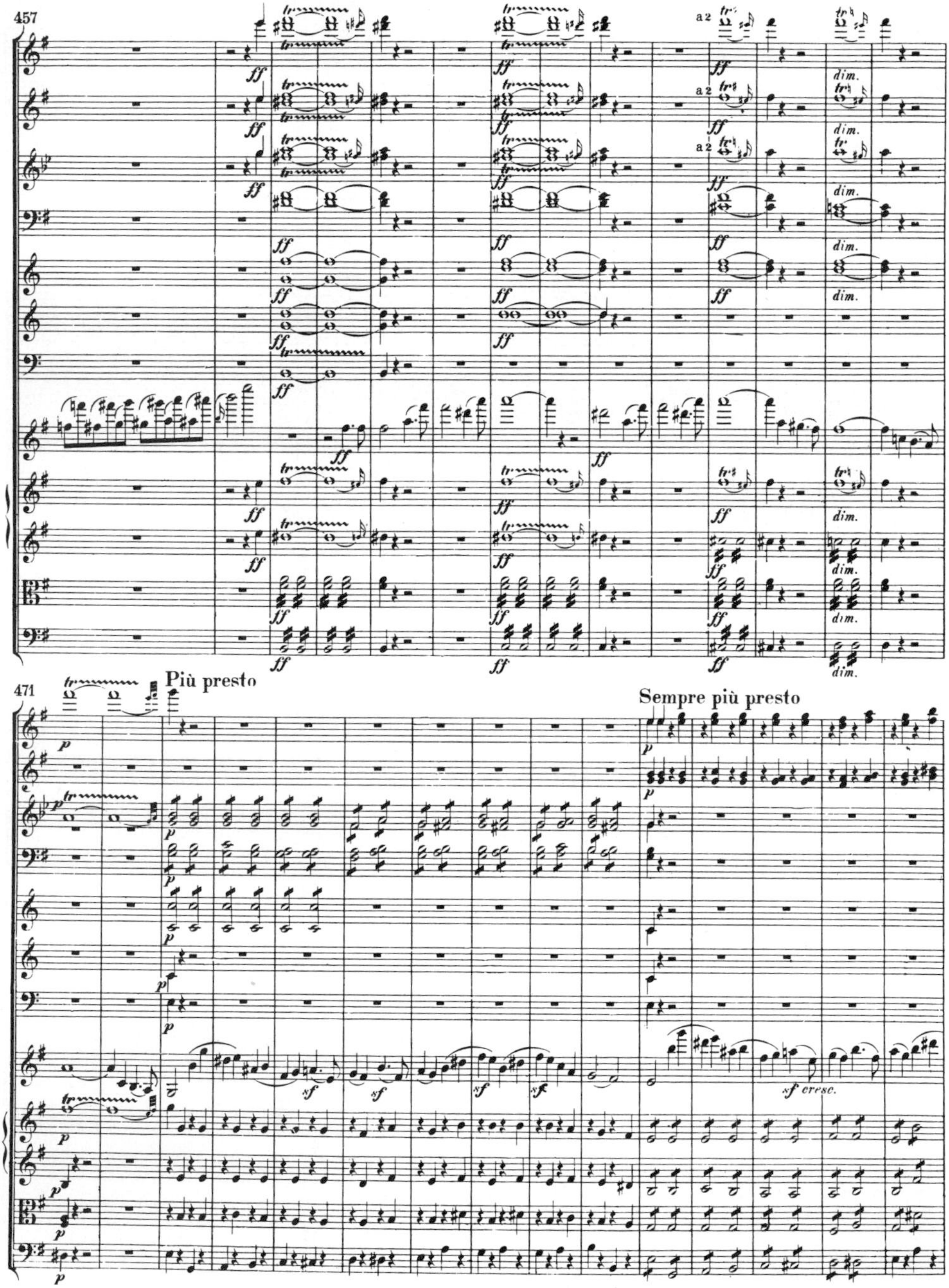
457
471
Più presto
Sempre più presto

Presto

20
cresc.
cresc.
p
cresc.
dim.
p
f
f
f
26
p
p
p
p
arco
arco
arco
arco
p
p
p

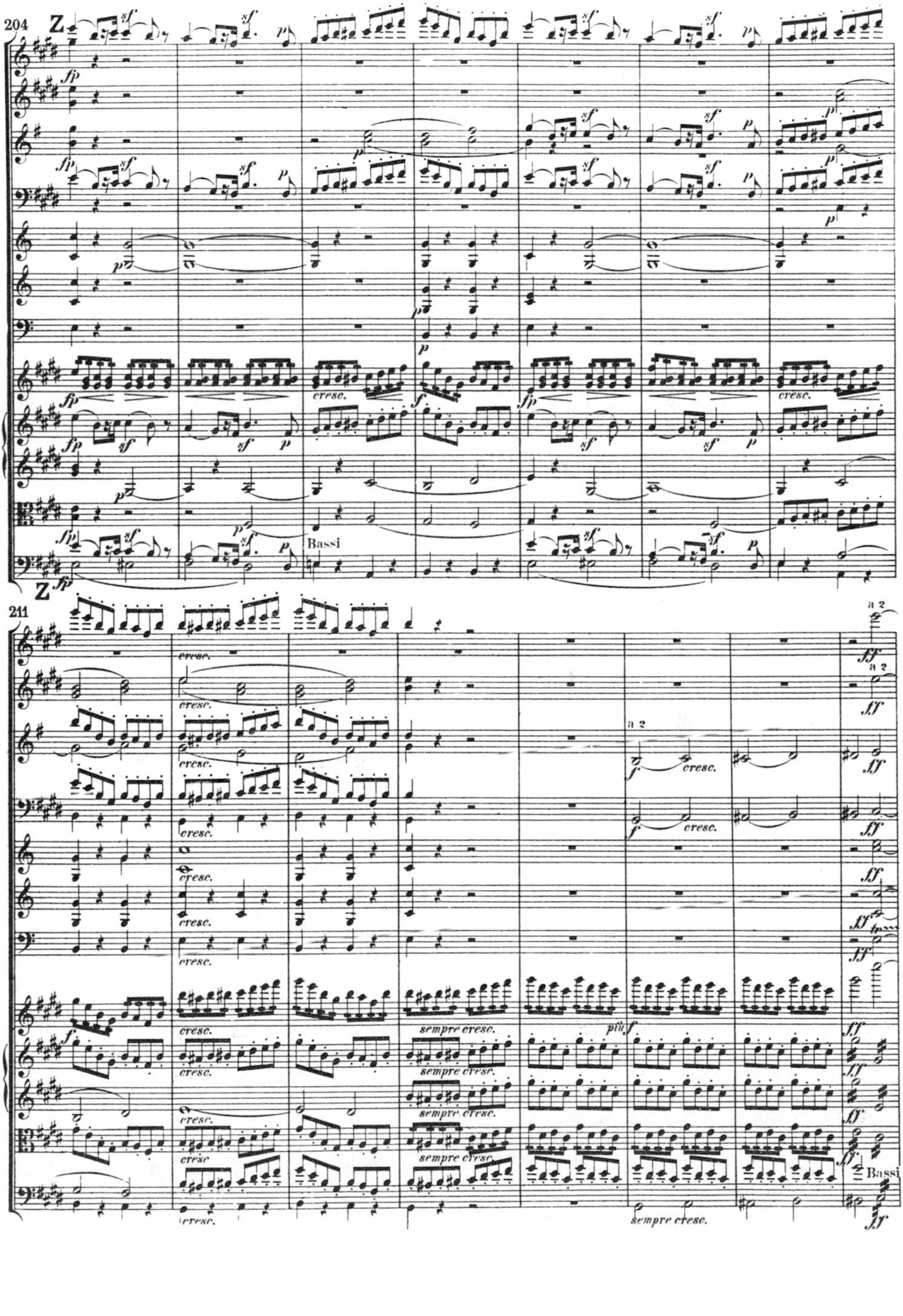
204
Z
fp
sf
p
cresc.
Bassi
211
a 2
ff
f
sempre cresc.
più f
Bassi

Robert Schumann (1810–1856)

CONCERTO FOR PIANO AND ORCHESTRA
IN A MINOR, OP. 54

(1845)

INSTRUMENTATION

2 Flutes (*Fl.*)
2 Oboes (*Ob.*)
2 Clarinets (*Cl.*) in A, B♭ (*B*)
2 Bassoons (*Fag.*)

2 Horns (*Cor.*) in C, A, F, E
2 Trumpets (*Tr.*) in C
Timpani (*Timp.*) in A, E, C, G

Solo Piano

Violin I
Violin II
Viola
Cello
Bass

490

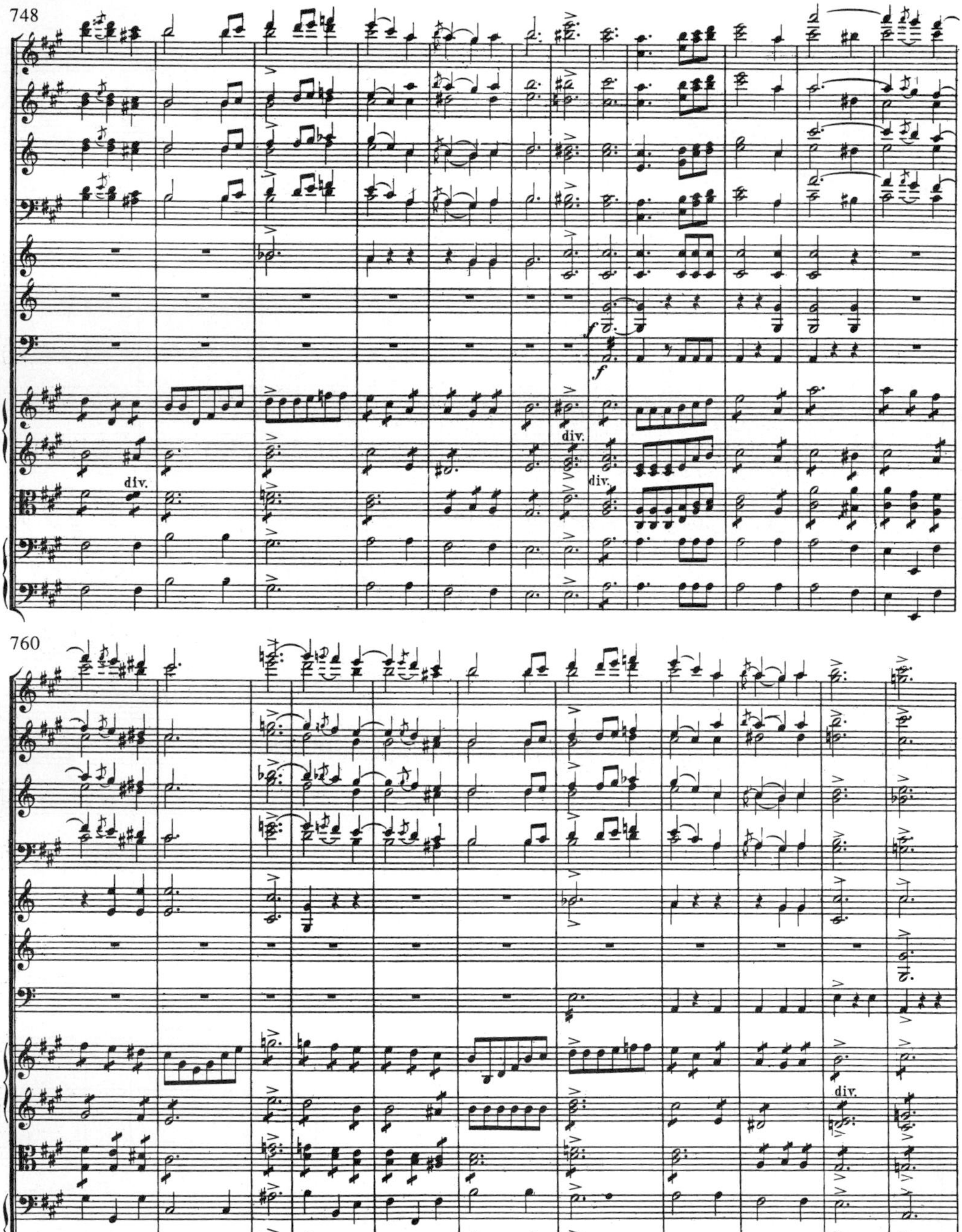
748
f
f
div.
div.
760
div.

943

952

961

Franz Liszt *(1811–1886)*

CONCERTO NO. 1 FOR PIANO AND

ORCHESTRA IN E♭ MAJOR

(1849, revised: 1853, 1856)

INSTRUMENTATION

1 Piccolo (*Kl. Fl.*)
2 Flutes (*Fl.*)
2 Oboes (*Ob.*)
2 Clarinets (*Klar.*) in B♭ (*B*), A
2 Bassoons (*Fag.*)

2 Horns (*Hr.*) in E♭
2 Trumpets (*Tr.*) in E♭
2 Tenor Trombones (*Pos.*)
Bass Trombone (*Pos.*)
Timpani (*Pk.*) in B♭ (*B*), F, E♭ (*Es*)
Cymbals (*Becken*)
Triangle (*Trgl.*)

Solo Piano

Violin I
Violin II
Viola
Cello
Bass

239

246

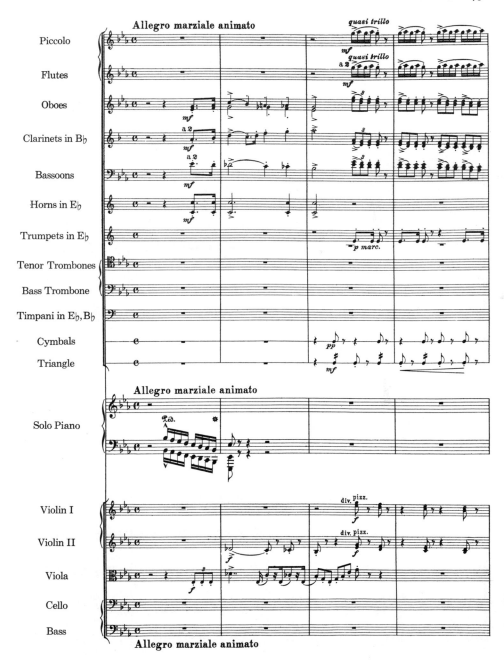

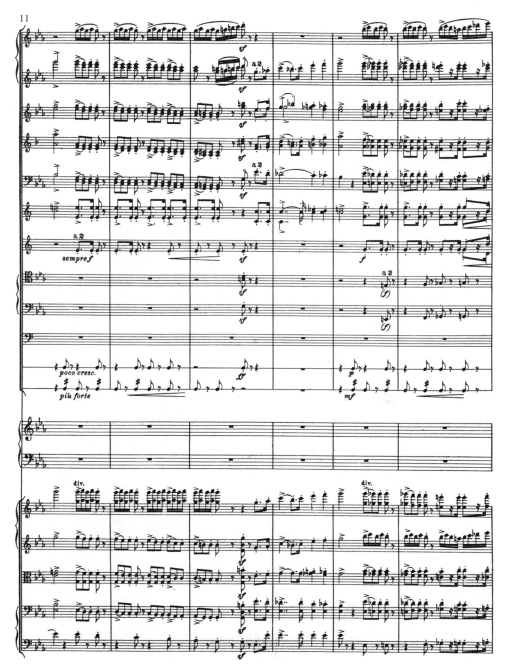

133

147

153

Peter Ilyich Tchaikovsky (1840–1893)

CONCERTO NO. 1 FOR PIANO AND ORCHESTRA IN B♭ MINOR, OP. 23

(1875)

INSTRUMENTATION

2 Flutes (*Fl.*)
2 Oboes (*Ob.*)
2 Clarinets (*Klar.*) in B♭
2 Bassoons (*Fag.*)

4 Horns (*Hr.*) in F
2 Trumpets (*Trpt.*) in F
3 Trombones (*Pos.*)
Timpani (*Pk.*) in A♭ (*As*), D♭ (*Des*), E♭ (*Es*), F, G, B♭ (*B*), B (*H*), G♭ (*Ges*)

Solo Piano (*Pfte.*)

Violin I (*Viol. I*)
Violin II (*Viol. II*)
Viola
Cello (*Vcll.*)
Bass (*K.-B.*)

*) The performance of the large part of the cadenza is *ad libitum*. Leaving same out one should pass on from sign *) to sign §

Johannes Brahms (1833–1897)

CONCERTO FOR VIOLIN AND ORCHESTRA

IN D MAJOR, OP. 77

(1 8 7 8)

INSTRUMENTATION

2 Flutes (*Fl.*)
2 Oboes (*Ob.*)
2 Clarinets (*Klar.*) in A, B♭ (*B*)
2 Bassoons (*Fag.*)

4 Horns (*Hr.*) in D, E, F
2 Trumpets (*Trpt.*) in D
Timpani (*Pk.*) in D, A

Solo Violin (*Solo*)

Violin I (*1. Viol.*)
Violin II (*2. Viol.*)
Viola (*Br.*)
Cello (*Vcl.*)
Bass (*K.-B.*)

Johannes Brahms

CONCERTO NO. 2 FOR PIANO AND ORCHESTRA IN B♭ MAJOR, OP. 83

(1881)

INSTRUMENTATION

2 Flutes (*Fl.*)
  II doubles on Piccolo (*Kl. Fl.*)
2 Oboes *(Ob.)*
2 Clarinets *(Klar.)* in B♭ *(B)*
2 Bassoons (*Fag.*)

4 Horns (*Hr.*) in B♭ basso (*B*), F, D
2 Trumpets (*Trpt.*) in B♭ (*B*), D
Timpani (*Pk.*) in B♭ (*B*), F, D, A

Solo Piano (*Klav.*)

Violin I (*1. Viol.*)
Violin II (*2. Viol.*)
Viola (*Br.*)
Cello (*Vcl.*)
Bass (*K.-B.*)

Antonín Dvořák (1841–1904)

CONCERTO FOR CELLO AND ORCHESTRA

IN B MINOR, OP. 104

(1895)

INSTRUMENTATION

2 Flutes (*Fl.*)
2 Oboes (*Ob.*)
2 Clarinets (*Cl.*) in A
2 Bassoons (*Fg.*)
2 Bassoons (*Fag.*)

3 Horns (*Cor.*) in C, D, E, F
2 Trumpets (*Tr.*) in E
2 Tenor Trombones (*Trb.*)
Bass Trombone (*Trb. b.*)
Tuba (*Tb.*)
Timpani (*Timp.*)

Solo Cello (*Vlc. Solo*)

Violin I (*Vl. I*)
Violin II (*Vl. II*)
Viola (*Vla.*)
Cello (*Vlc.*)
Bass (*Cb.*)

260

300

Un poco più animato

Appendix

Reading an Orchestral Score

CLEFS

The music for some instruments is written in clefs other than the familiar treble and bass. In the following example, middle C is shown in the four clefs used in orchestral scores:

The *alto clef* is primarily used in viola parts. The *tenor clef* is employed for cello, bassoon, and trombone parts when these instruments play in a high register.

TRANSPOSING INSTRUMENTS

The music for some instruments is customarily written at a pitch different from their actual sound. The following list, with examples, shows the main transposing instruments and the degree of transposition.

Instrument	*Transposition*	*Written Note*	*Actual Sound*
Piccolo, Celesta	sound an octave higher than written		
Trumpet in F	sound a fourth higher than written		
Trumpet in E	sound a major third higher than written		

Instrument	Transposition	Written Note	Actual Sound

Clarinet in E♭,
Trumpet in E♭ — sound a minor third higher than written

Trumpet in D — sound a major second higher than written

Clarinet in B♭,
Trumpet in B♭,
Cornet in B♭ — sound a major second lower than written

Clarinet in A,
Horn in A
Cornet in A — sound a minor third lower than written

English horn,
Horn in F — sound a fifth lower than written

Horn in E — sound a minor sixth lower than written

Horn in E♭ — sound a major sixth lower than written

Horn in D — sound a major seventh lower than written

Horn in C,
Double bass — sound an octave lower than written

Horn in B♭ basso — sound a major ninth lower than written